THE AUTHENTIC GUITAR STYLE OF

JOHN DENVER

Cherry Lane Music
ACOUSTIC GUITAR SERIES

Transcribed by Peter Seckel and Kenn Chipkin
Edited by Mark Phillips
Art Direction: Alisa Hill
Production Manager: Daniel Rosenbaum
Administration: Deborah Poletto
ISBN: 0-89524-376-8

READING GUITAR TABLATURE

Tablature is a six-line staff that graphically represents the guitar fingerboard, with the top line indicating the highest sounding string (high E).

1st string - High E
2nd string -   B
3rd string -   G
4th string -   D
5th string -   A
6th string - Low   E

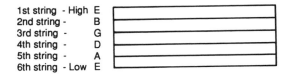

By placing a number on the appropriate line, the string and fret of any note can be indicated. The number 0 represents an open string. For example:

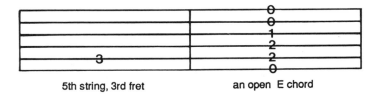

5th string, 3rd fret   an open E chord

PERFORMANCE NOTES

Stem Direction

In music of two or more parts, notes with downward stems are played by the thumb; notes with upward stems are played by the fingers; a note with a double stem (up and down) is played by the thumb.

Left-Hand Techniques

A hammer-on is indicated by the letter H. A pull-off is indicated by the letter P. A slide is indicated by the letters *sl.*

CONTENTS

TAKE ME HOME, COUNTRY ROADS

Words and Music by
Bill Danoff, Taffy Nivert
and John Denver

ma,_____ take__ me home,_____ coun - try roads._____

I hear her voice, in the morn-in' hour she calls_____ me. The ra - di - o_____ re - minds__ me of my home far a - way.__ And driv - in' down__ the road__ I get a

feel - in' that I should have been home yes - ter - day, _____ yes - ter - day.

D.S. al Coda Coda

Coun - try roads, ___

_____ Take_ me home, ___

coun - try roads. _____ Take_ me home, ___

coun - try roads. _____

ROCKY MOUNTAIN HIGH

Words and Music by
John Denver and Mike Taylor

*To play along with recording, place capo at 2nd fret.

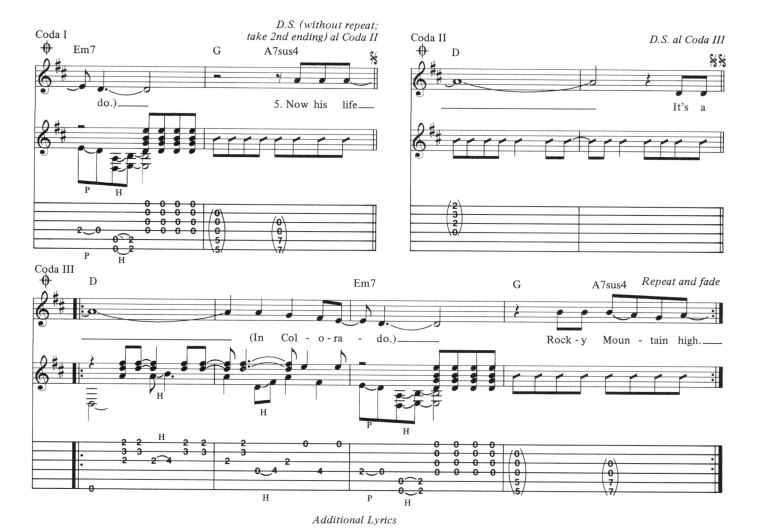

Additional Lyrics

2. When he first came to the mountains his life was far away,
   On the road and hangin' by a song.
   But the string's already broken and he doesn't really care.
   It keeps changin' fast, and it don't last for long. *(To 1st Chorus)*

3. He climbed cathedral mountains, he saw silver clouds below.
   He saw everything as far as you can see.
   And they say that he got crazy once and he tried to touch the sun,
   And he lost a friend but kept his memory.

4. Now he walks in quiet solitude the forests and the streams,
   Seeking grace in every step he takes.
   His sight has turned inside himself to try and understand
   The serenity of a clear blue mountain lake.

   2nd Chorus:
   And the Colorado Rocky Mountain high,
   I've seen it rainin' fire in the sky.
   You can talk to God and listen to the casual reply.
   Rocky Mountain high. (In Colorado.)
   Rocky Mountain high. (In Colorado.)

5. Now his life is full of wonder but his heart still knows some fear
   Of a simple thing he cannot comprehend.
   Why they try to tear the mountains down to bring in a couple more,
   More people, more scars upon the land.

   3rd Chorus:
   And the Colorado Rocky Mountain high,
   I've seen it rainin' fire in the sky.
   I know he'd be a poorer man if he never saw an eagle fly.
   Rocky Mountain high.

   4th Chorus:
   It's a Colorado Rocky Mountain high.
   I've seen it rainin' fire in the sky.
   Friends around the campfire and everybody's high.
   Rock Mountain high. (In Colorado.)

ANNIE'S SONG

Words and Music by
John Denver

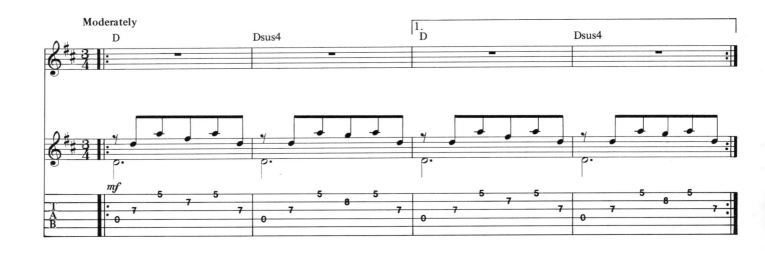

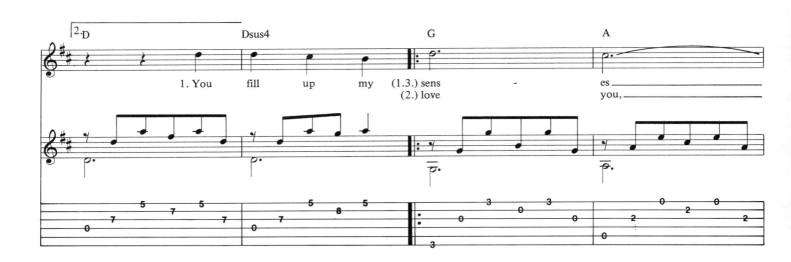

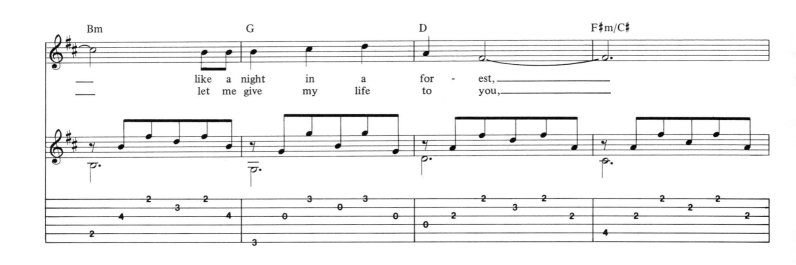

*Sing small notes 2nd and 3rd times.

I'M SORRY

Words and Music by
John Denver

15

for liv - in' with - out___ you.___

Mm,___

mm,

mm.___

SUNSHINE ON MY SHOULDERS

Words by John Denver
Music by John Denver,
Mike Taylor and Dick Kniss

*To play along with recording, place capo at 3rd fret.

21

LEAVING ON A JET PLANE

Words and Music by
John Denver

Additional Lyrics

2. There's so many times I've let you down,
   So many times I've played around,
   I tell you now they don't mean a thing.
   Every place I go I'll think of you,
   Every song I sing I'll sing for you,
   When I come back I'll bring your wedding ring.

   Chorus

3. Now the time has come to leave you,
   One more time let me kiss you,
   Then close your eyes, I'll be on my way.
   Dream about the days to come,
   When I won't have to leave alone,
   About the times I won't have to say:

   Chorus

POEMS, PRAYERS AND PROMISES

Words and Music by
John Denver

1. I've been late-ly think-in'_____ a-bout my life's time,_____
2.3.4. *See additional lyrics*

all the things I've done and how it's been. And

I can't help be-liev-in' in ____ my own mind,

26

28

Additional Lyrics

2. I've seen a lot of sunshine, slept out in the rain.
   Spent a night or two all on my own.
   I've known my lady's pleasures, had myself some friends,
   Spent a time or two in my own home.

   Bridge

   Chorus

3. The days they pass so quickly now, the nights are seldom long,
   Time around me whispers when it's cold.
   The changes somehow frighten me, still I have to smile,
   It turns me on to think of growing old.

4. For though my life's been good to me there's still so much to do,
   So many things my mind has never known.
   I'd like to raise a family, I'd like to sail away,
   And dance across the mountains on the moon.

   Bridge

   Chorus

BACK HOME AGAIN

Words and Music by
John Denver

1. There's a storm a- cross the val- ley, clouds are roll- in' in, the af- ter- noon is heav- y on your shoul-

2.3.4. See additional lyrics

ders. _____ There's a truck out on __ the four - lane __ a

mile or more a - way, __ the whin - in' of __ his wheels __ just makes it

Play 1st time only (To 2nd verse) | Play 2nd, 3rd and 4th times only

cold - er. _____ 2. He's an __

Chorus

Hey, it's good to be back home __ a - gain. _____

D.S. al Coda

Coda

Additional Lyrics

2. He's an hour away from ridin' on your prayers up in the sky,
   And ten days on the road are barely gone.
   There's a fire softly burnin', supper's on the stove,
   But it's the light in your eyes that makes him warm.

   Chorus

3. There's all the news to tell him, how'd you spend your time,
   And what's the latest thing the neighbors say?
   And your mother called last Friday, "Sunshine" made her cry,
   And you felt the baby move just yesterday.

   Chorus

   Bridge

4. It's the sweetest thing I know of just spending time with you,
   It's the little things that make a house a home,
   Like a fire softly burnin' and supper on the stove
   And the light in your eyes that makes me warm.

   Chorus

FOLLOW ME

Words and Music by
John Denver

GOODBYE AGAIN

Words and Music by
John Denver

Medium tempo

1. It's five o'-clock this morn - ing and the sun is on the rise. There's
2.3. *See additional lyrics*

frost - ing on the win - dow-pane and sor - row in your eyes. The

stars are fad - ing qui - et - ly, night is near - ly gone. And so you turn a - way

from me, and tears— be- gin to come.— And it's good- bye — a- gain.— I'm—

sor - ry to— be leav - ing you. Good - bye a - gain,—

'cause if you did -n't know,— it's good - bye a - gain,— and I wish you— could tell—

— me, why— do we al - ways fight— when I have to go? _____ 2. It

3rd time to Coda

39

Em   Am7

It's an - y - one _____ who'll lis - ten _____ to me sing. ____

D   D.S. al Coda   Coda

rit.

Additional Lyrics

2. It seems a shame to leave you now, the days are soft and warm.
   I long to lay me down again and hold you in my arms.
   I long to kiss the tears away and give you back your smile,
   But other voices beckon me, and for a little while:

   Chorus

   Bridge

3. If your hours are empty now, who am I to blame?
   You think if I were always here, our love would be the same?
   As it is, the time we have is worth the time alone,
   And lying by your side, the greatest peace I've ever known.

   Chorus

THIS OLD GUITAR

Words and Music by
John Denver

* Use thumb

1. This old gui-tar taught me to sing
2.3. *See additional lyrics*

a love song, showed me how to laugh and how to cry.

* To play along with recording, place capo at 2nd fret.

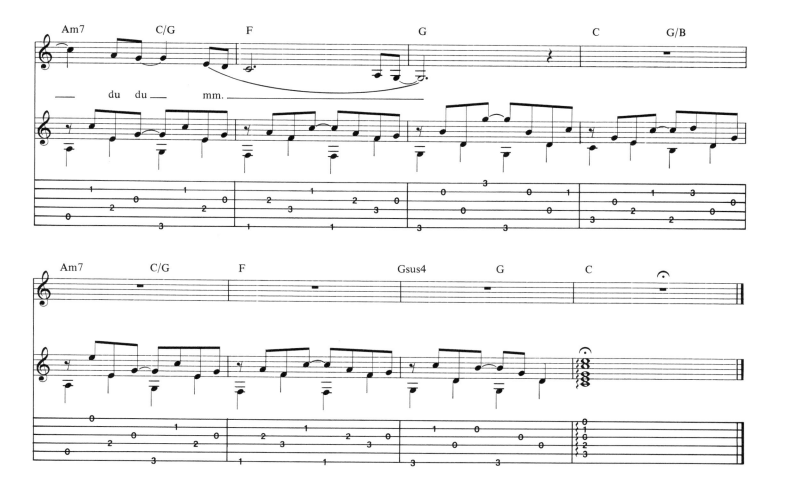

du du __ mm. _____

Additional Lyrics

2. This old guitar gave me my lovely lady,
   It opened up her eyes and ears to me.
   It brought us close together, and I guess it broke her heart.
   It opened up the space for us to be.
   What a lovely place and a lovely space to be.

3. This old guitar gave me my life, my living,
   All the things you know I love to do,
   To serenade the stars that shine from a sunny mountainside,
   And most of all to sing my songs for you.
   I love to sing my songs for you, *(etc.)*

MY SWEET LADY

Words and Music by
John Denver

Additional Lyrics

2. Lady, are you happy, do you feel the way I do,
   Are there meanings that you've never seen before?
   Lady, my sweet lady, I just can't believe it's true,
   And it's like I've never ever loved before.
   Close your eyes, *(etc.)*

3. Lady, are you crying, do the tears belong to me?
   Did you think our time together was all gone?
   Lady, my sweet lady, I'm as close as I can be,
   And I swear to you our time has just begun.